FAR OUT
FABLES

raintree

a Capstone company — publishers for children

INTRODUCING...

GRIGORE

ION

MR & MRS
COJOCARU

OLGA

ALEXANDRU

IN...

Raintree is an imprint of Capstone
Global Library Limited, a company
incorporated in England and Wales
having its registered office at 264
Banbury Road, Oxford, OX2 7DY –
Registered company number: 6695582

www.raintree.co.uk
myorders@raintree.co.uk

Text and illustrations © Capstone
Global Library Limited 2018.
The moral rights of the proprietor
have been asserted.

Designed by Hilary Wacholz
Edited by Abby Huff
Lettered by Jaymes Reed

ISBN 978 1 474 75031 8
21 20 19 18 17
10 9 8 7 6 5 4 3 2 1

British Library Cataloguing in
Publication Data: A full catalogue
record for this book is available
from the British Library.

Printed and bound in China.

FAR OUT FABLES

THE BOY WHO CRIED VAMPIRE

A GRAPHIC NOVEL

BY BENJAMIN HARPER

ILLUSTRATED BY ALEX LOPEZ

In Transylvania, a small village once sat at the base of a mysterious mountain.

High atop that mountain was an ancient, sinister castle.

No villagers travelled to the castle. No one stayed out past sunset.

Let's go inside, little ones.

For legends told of a terrifying vampire who lived in the castle.

One who would surely snack on any villager or traveller who stayed out after nightfall.

And that vampire's name was. . .

GRIGORE THE DREADED

The villagers lived in fear of the terrible vampire – well, all except one.

Ion Cojocaru wasn't scared. He thought the village was boring.

ZOMBIE

DEAD?

THE MUMMY

÷Sigh÷

To make life more exciting, Ion loved to play pranks.

EEEEEE!

And he was always making up wild stories.

...and then the werewolf gobbled up the sheep! Mrs Gabor went without wool for an entire season.

When he wasn't telling tall tales, Ion liked to watch old scary films.

He was fascinated by any type of monster, ghost or ghoul.

Most of all, though, Ion loved vampires.

I vant to suck your blood!

One night, after watching a vampire film, Ion got an idea.

Hehehe! I can't wait!

Time to put my plan into *action.*

He took a deep breath. Then cried –

VAMPIRE!

VAMPIRE!

VAMPIRE!

Please, help! *Grigore* is after me!

12

The next night, Ion was bored – again. He had read all his comics. There was nothing on TV.

Not even any monster films!

And then . . . an idea!

Best. Prank. *EVER!* It'd be wrong *not* to do it.

Perfect!

14

You **still** fell for it!

Just try it again and see what happens.

You have fooled us for the **last time**, little Ion. No more of your silly tricks!

Yeah!

Can we go back to bed now?

Once again, Ion's embarrassed parents led him home.

Come on, you have to **admit** that was a brilliant prank.

That's it! You're grounded until you are thirty-five!

⊰ Sigh ⊱

The next night, Ion was in his room doing his homework. Suddenly he heard . . .

SCRAAAATCH!

SCRAAAAATCH!

SCRAATCH!

. . . at his window!

Oh, wow. Could it be . . . a *real* vampire?!

After all, it's dark. *Everybody* knows vampires come out at night to feed.

And they love fresh blood. Humans are basically vampire *juice cartons!*

And the villagers said they wouldn't help me again. So if the vampire is looking for a meal, I'll be easy pickings...

I'm *DOOMED.*

But maybe it's *nothing.* I'll just check and get it over with!

20

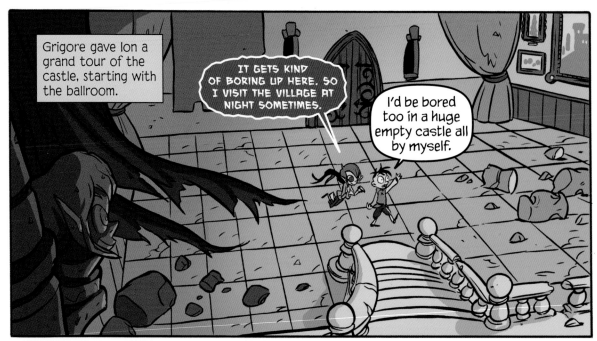

Grigore gave Ion a grand tour of the castle, starting with the ballroom.

IT GETS KIND OF BORING UP HERE. SO I VISIT THE VILLAGE AT NIGHT SOMETIMES.

I'd be bored too in a huge empty castle all by myself.

I WAS HIDING IN THE SHADOWS WHEN YOU WERE *PRETENDING* TO BE BITTEN.

HA! WHAT A *GREAT* PRANK! THE KETCHUP WAS A NICE TOUCH.

Thanks! I thought so too. The villagers don't appreciate my humour.

So, Grigore... can vampires turn into *bats?* Is that a real thing?

OF COURSE!

P000F!

Amazing!

IT *IS* PRETTY AWESOME — EXCEPT FOR THE *FLEAS.*

WAIT TILL YOU SEE WHAT'S IN THE CRYPT.

Oh wow – a *genuine* crypt?!

This is so *COOL!* It's much less creepy than I expected.

I MAY BE UNDEAD, BUT I STILL LIKE TO HAVE FUN. WANT TO PLAY?

IT!

Um...hanging out with a vampire is only like my *DREAM.*

Grigore showed Ion his rare comic collection and his vintage toys. The two played games throughout the night.

Ion was having so much fun that he lost track of the time.

I'll just take a quick nap, then I'll go home...

The next day . . .

Help! Help! Ion is missing!

Ion isn't in his room. And his windows were open!

My poor little boy! Grigore has taken him. I know it!

I heard Ion shouting about Grigore last night. I *suppose* he did sound pretty scared.

I heard him too. But I thought it was another joke!

Uh-oh.

26

They finally arrived at the castle.

Smash the door in!

CRUNCH!

They ran through the great hall.

And straight to the crypt!

Shhh. We must be careful, or Grigore may attack us!

What kind of a crypt is this? It's just a load of *kids' stuff.*

Here it is. The coffin of *Grigore the Dreaded!*

We will end his reign of terror once and for all!

STOP!

29

Grigore isn't *deadly* – he's lonely! He wants to be our friend!

Huh?

Have you gone *mad*, Ion? Grigore is our *enemy*!

You're *okay*!

But as the sun set, the coffin creaked open and out popped . . .

GRIGORE THE DREADED!!!

Wait...this is *Grigore?*

No, that's just a kid in a bad costume and Halloween makeup!

Another prank? You've really outdone yourself, Ion.

Who's this *other* kid? His parents should ground him.

Seriously?! You guys, look around you.

Crypts, old coffins, *BLUE SKIN!* This is *real.* I'm telling the truth!

I THOUGHT I WAS A *LITTLE SCARY.*

I guess "Grigore the Dreaded" is just a *myth.* Because there are *definitely no* vampires here!

So many lies! I say Ion should clean the stables for the rest of his life as punishment.

But Mum, he really is a vampire!

I'm sure he is, sweetie. Now let's get you home.

31

The villagers searched the castle from top to bottom. But they didn't find any signs that a real vampire lived there - even though one did.

So they no longer believed in the legend of Grigore the Dreaded. The dark held no terror for them now.

Ugh, that old castle should be torn down!

What a lovely evening.

Ion rarely got bored anymore. He even stopped pulling pranks.

After all, he was too busy hanging out with his new best friend.

Then how about the vampire says, "I vant to suck your blood"?

YEAH, COOL! SPEAKING OF BLOOD...

I'M ALL OUT OF BEETROOT JUICE... AND I'M STILL HUNGRY.

BWAHAHAHA!

EEK!

VAMPIRE

JUST KIDDING!

Whoa, haha! Good one, Grigore!

Plus Grigore still had fun playing his own pranks every now and then.

That kept Ion's life exciting enough.

ALL ABOUT FABLES

A fable is a short tale that teaches the reader a lesson about life, often with animal characters. Most fables were first told thousands of years ago by a Greek storyteller called Aesop. At the end of a fable, there's almost always a moral (a fancy word for lesson) stated very clearly, so you don't miss it. Yes, fables can be a bit bossy, but they usually give pretty good advice. Read on to learn more about Aesop's original fable and its moral. Can you spot any other lessons?

THE BOY WHO CRIED WOLF

A shepherd boy is watching the village's flock of sheep. It's a boring job, so he decides to make some fun. "Wolf! Wolf!" he cries. All the villagers rush in to save their animals. But there's no wolf to be seen! The crowd storms back home. Later, the boy cries wolf again. The villagers come running – only to find the boy is still joking. One day, a wolf really DOES appear. "Help! Wolf!" the boy yells. This time no one comes. When the boy isn't back by sunset, the villagers go to check on him. They find the young shepherd crying. "A wolf attacked and frightened away all the sheep!" the boy says. "Why didn't you come?" The villagers answer, "We thought it was another silly joke!" But as everyone heads home, they promise to help the boy find the lost sheep in the morning.

THE MORAL

NO ONE BELIEVES A LIAR,
EVEN WHEN HE'S TELLING THE TRUTH
(In other words, people
won't trust you if
you're always lying!)

A **FAR OUT** GUIDE TO THE FABLE'S BATTY TWISTS!

Instead of fibbing about a hungry wolf, Ion tells tall tales about bloodsucking vampires!

No one knows where the shepherd boy's village was. Ion's home is in Transylvania, home to many fictional monsters and ghouls!

In the original fable, a flock of sheep go missing. In this version, the villagers promise to help find the lost *boy*!

We don't know if the original boy ever learned his lesson. In this far-out tale, Ion now spends his time hanging out with Grigore and writing stories instead of telling lies.

VISUAL QUESTIONS

In your own words, describe how Ion used the ketchup in his prank. (Look back to pages 14-16 if you need help.)

The light bulb above Ion's head is a symbol -- a visible sign of something invisible, like thoughts or feelings. What does the light bulb symbolize? Try to find other symbols used in the story. (Hint: Look above Olga's head on page 16.)

In graphic novels, you can tell a lot about how characters feel just by looking at the art. How do the villagers feel here? What is it about the art that makes you think that?

4

We don't see what Grigore looks like until page 23. Why do think the creators chose to do this? What feeling does it create?

5

It was a drill. Everybody should be *thanking* me!

You're grounded for a *month*, young man!

The original fable warns readers that no one believes liars, even when they tell the truth. What do you think Ion learned at the end of this story? Why?

AUTHOR

Benjamin Harper has worked as an editor at Lucasfilm LTD. and DC Comics. He currently lives in Los Angeles, USA, where he writes, watches monster films and hangs out with his cat Edith Bouvier Beale III. His other books include *Obsessed With Star Wars*, *Thank You, Superman!* and *Hansel & Gretel & Zombies*.

ILLUSTRATOR

Alex Lopez became a professional illustrator and comic book artist in 2001, but he's been drawing ever since he can remember. Lopez's pieces have been published in many countries, including the UK, USA, Spain, France, Italy, Belgium and Turkey. He's also worked on a wide variety of projects from illustrated books to video games to marketing . . . but what he loves most is making comic books.

GLOSSARY

appreciate enjoy, value or understand something or someone

crypt underground chamber, often used as a burial place for the dead (or undead!)

dreaded greatly feared and makes you very worried

embarrass feel silly or foolish in front of others

flea tiny bloodsucking insect often found on animals

legend story passed down through the years that may not be completely true

prank playful trick; sometimes a prank may annoy others or cause harm

reign time during which someone has power and influence over others

rescue save from harm or trouble

sinister looking evil or harmful

tall tales stories that have extraordinary or unbelievable details but are told as if they were true

vintage from the past

THE MORAL OF THE STORY IS... EPIC!

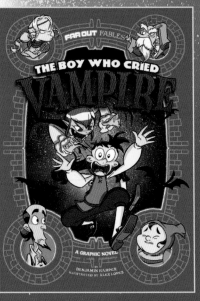

FAR OUT FABLES